The Thing
That Came To Dinner

THE THING
THAT CAME TO DINNER

James Carney

Unseen Things

2018
www.unseenhour.com

First Printing: 2018
ISBN-13: 978-1981938872
ISBN-10: 1981938877

Unseen Things
Studio 2, Mainyard Studios, 90 Wallis Road
London E9 5LN
www.unseenhour.com

Dramatis Personae

MACKENZIE CAULDWELL

ALEC MAURUS — University friend of Don.

DON STUART — Mackenzie's cousin. Master of the house.

MRS. AUDREY CAULDWELL — Mackenzie's mother. Don's Aunt.

DR. SHERIDAN BEWLEY — Old family friend of the Cauldwells.

ELIZABETH VAN WALL — Childhood friend of Don.

The following characters are played as puppets,
or by the any actor putting on a key costume element:

ASQUITH - The butler.
MRS. NAVIDSON - The housekeeper.
MRS. COPPER - The cook.
BELLEROPHON - Mrs. Cauldwell's dog.
THE THING - A monster.
VARIOUS SPIRITS

Note:
The special effects, props and set will have a homemade look. For the set this will be largely mimicking the German Expressionist style of films like The Cabinet Of Dr. Caligari, but for the more organic sort of special effect prop it will be more in the style of John Carpenter's The Thing, his other films, or perhaps David Cronenberg's body horror.

Each time something impossible is described in the stage directions, it should be performed by the Spirit characters (or personas of the performers) as some kind of puppetry. Preferably using various household objects.

The drinks that Don mixes throughout should be stirred cocktails with ice, strained into stemmed glasses, so that they look appealing and make a little noise, but not as much as a shaken cocktail. Martinis would fit the bill.

Original Cast
VAULT Festival 2018

MAC	–	**Karla Marie Sweet**
MAURUS	–	**Angus Dunican**
DON	–	**James Carney**
MRS. CAULDWELL	–	**Balvinder Sopal**
BEWLEY	–	**Sami Abu Wardeh**
VAN WALL	–	**Molly Beth Morossa**

Kickstarter Backers:
Kathryn Gardner, Maya Korn, Ekaterina Krasnova, Simon Farid,
Emily Garland, Clare Wadlow, Anthony Clark Brown, Duncan Hendry,
Gordon Wallis, Katie Correll, Kate Mawby, Thomas Jancis,
Emily Walters, Rebecca Crookshank, Andrew Huggett,
Scarlett Plouviez Comnas, Brice Stratford, Dan & Jenny Thompson,
Holly Casey, Samantha Whates, Maggie Turner, Mat Burt,
Emily Parrett, Tim Wilson, Georgia Clarke-Day, Perrine Davies,
Canavan Connolly, Sam Thompson, Fiona Thraille,
Christopher D Overbeck, Jen Sugden, CJ Wilckens, Ben Hogan,
Nic Lamont, Andrew Thompson, Barry Shapiro, Sean Curtis-Ward,
David Maxwell Krakowski, Greer Dale Foulkes, Sara Ann Hope,
Max Kreisky, Laurel Murray, Luke Graham,
Maddi Sainsbury, Joe Ewens, James King

Directed and Produced by James Carney

Music by The Unrecorded
Movement Consultant: Rachele Rapisardi
Sound Design: Óðinn Örn Hilmarsson
Lighting Design: Gemma Leader
Assistant Producers: Joseph Cullen and Jamie McInnes

Executive Producer:
Gordon Wallis

Prelude

Spirits move about the space in semi-darkness. They move objects around, arranging chairs, hat-stands, the fireplace. It's a living room. They seem to construct the actors, draw them onto stage as if hypnotised. Arrange their bodies into elegant, character specific poses, and set them in motion like clockwork toys. The characters wander the space indistinctly - sleep-walking in slow motion and with exaggerated elegance - vacant, entranced, submarine.

OVERTURE: FROM THE DEPTHS

The spirits pick up objects and construct a small dog - BELLEROPHON.

BELLEROPHON is a small, confrontational dog - a Pomeranian. He scampers about the living room, doing things that dogs do. After a few moments he finds and knocks over a bucket of ice. He licks the ice enthusiastically.

ASQUITH [VAN WALL], the butler enters, sees BELLEROPHON eating the ice, and shoos him away. ASQUITH scoops the ice from the floor, replaces it in the bucket. Inspects the ice distastefully, and takes it away, shaking his head.

A short dance sequence ensues where BELLEROPHON moves amongst the other characters.

At its conclusion, MACKENZIE (MAC) is left alone on stage, standing by the fireplace.

BELLEROPHON re-enters. Stops and looks at her ominously, from across the room. She notices him and rolls her eyes.

BELLEROPHON checks that they are alone, then transforms from a dog into a much larger and more savage monster. MAC is horrified and amazed as it advances on her. She grabs a fire-iron and beats at the monster. It collapses into a heap and lies still.

1

MAC steps back very surprised.

The crumpled heap that used to be BELLEROPHON stirs and begins to rise up. MAC beats at it again, then flicks the corpse into the fire, where it writhes, burns, screams and finally lies still.

Act I

MRS. CAULDWELL, MAC, DON, VAN WALL

MRS. CAULDWELL

　　My poor darling Belly! My little Bellerophon! You never liked
　　him you ungrateful girl!

MAC

　　Mother, there was something wrong with him! I'm sorry but
　　there was something very, very wrong with him.

MRS. CAULDWELL

　　How could you possibly know that? Oh maybe if you'd studied
　　biology or medicine like I said. Don't you think you'd do better
　　with a job like that?

MAC

　　I'm sure, but I do already have a job. I think I'd rather continue
　　being a pilot - which, to most people, is quite impressive - than
　　completely retrain for a career in which I have no interest.

MRS. CAULDWELL

　　It's no good. My own daughter is a brutal murderer.

DON

　　This is all rather exciting. It's like a murder mystery. The six of
　　us all snowed in at my rural manor.

MAC

　　Please, Don.

DON

　　But it is! Allow me to exposit further: The phone lines down, no
　　hope of rescue until the morning at least, the suspects gather
　　after dinner in the wake of this atrocity, dreading the
　　inevitable thrilling cross-examination!

VAN WALL

　　Except that we already know whodunit.

MAC
>Van. Not you too.

DON
>Ah, yes. Not much of a mystery there.

VAN WALL
>The mystery's in the why!

DON
>Yes! What are their motives? Who are these strange and beautiful sophisticated people?

VAN WALL
>What secrets do they conceal? Are they who they say they are?

DON
>Would you like a drink?

VAN WALL
>Not entirely apposite, that one.

DON
>Says you.

MRS. CAULDWELL
>Don! Your high spirits are quite out of place! I am in mourning!

DON
>Ah. Yes. Sorry Aunt Aud. Callous of us. I forget how much you loved the poor brute. Do have a drink. Let's all have a drink. Asquith! Bring more ice!

>*DON mixes drinks for everyone.*

VAN WALL
>A couple more, Don, the men are coming back.

Enter DR. BEWLEY and MAURUS, with a horribly mutated dog corpse on a tray.

MAURUS
It's an absolute pleasure to work with you on this Dr. Bewley - strange though it is. As I say your work is quite an inspiration to me.

BEWLEY
Yes. You mentioned.

MAC
What happened to the dog? What was wrong with it?

MAURUS
Hm? Oh. You'd better explain, Doctor Bewley. I'm sure it would sound like madness coming from me.

BEWLEY
Hm. It's - interesting. We are in agreement that this - is not a dog.

MRS. CAULDWELL
Not a dog! Sheri! What can you possibly mean! Bellerophon is a most beautiful Pomeranian.

BEWLEY
Ah, yes. It should perhaps be stated, in addition, that this - is not Bellerophon.

DON
The plot thickens. Asquith! What the devil's taking so- Ah!

VAN WALL having gone to the hat stand and put on a clip-on shirtfront with bow-tie appears next to DON. She is now ASQUITH, the butler. He hands DON a bucket of ice. Scowling, DON continues to make drinks.

DON
Thank you, Asquith!

MAURUS
Doctor Bewley expresses it perfectly. Yes, these bits here look like your dog, but what's all this nonsense? It looks like nothing on Earth!

VAN WALL
It looks like it has hands! Don, look at these crazy little hands.

DON
No thank you.

MAC
The eyes. I noticed when it first... transformed... The anger. The malice.

MAURUS
It certainly seems like it's... not of this world.

MAC
So it's what? An alien?

MAURUS
Well, that's a bit of a leap. There's really no indication-

DON
Gosh! Aliens!

BEWLEY
From what we can tell it's some other creature that is - imitating - the dog. Or was. We're not quite sure how long it's been doing so.

MAURUS
Mac, or Mrs. Cauldwell, would you say that - you know - earlier... he was behaving normally?

MAC
That animal's behaviour could never be considered normal.

MRS. CAULDWELL
Mackenzie!

MAC
But it was its usual awful trembly self, until it started sprouting tentacles and extra teeth.

ASQUITH [VAN WALL]
> If I may, sir. Earlier this afternoon I did find the animal in question consuming the contents of an ice bucket.

DON
> Heavens Asquith. Not this ice, I hope.

ASQUITH [VAN WALL]
> No, sir. It was the bucket that you had me borrow from the Nygards.

DON
> The Norwegian ice. I see.

ASQUITH [VAN WALL]
> Adequately icy, sir, yes.

MRS. CAULDWELL
> Asquith, do you still have that bucket of ice? Perhaps we can discover what happened to my poor darling, Bellerophon.

ASQUITH [VAN WALL]
> I believe so, madam. It may have melted a little by now. I shall retrieve it.

> *VAN WALL removes ASQUITH's shirtfront and puts on MRS. COPPER's chef's hat.*

BEWLEY
> I'm so sorry this has happened, Audrey. I can't imagine...

MRS. CAULDWELL
> Well at least *you* have some empathy, Doctor.

MAC
> What was I supposed to do? Let it maul me?

MAURUS
> Oh, I think you were quite right.

MAC
> I'm glad I have your approval!

7

MRS. COPPER [VAN WALL] *(off)*
Ow Lord!

MAC
What now?

MRS. COPPER [VAN WALL] enters holding a severed dog's leg.

MRS. COPPER [VAN WALL]
Mr. Stuart, sir, you'll want to see this!

DON
If it's what I think it is Mrs. Copper I very much do not wish to see it.

MAURUS
Ha! It's a leg. That makes one... two... three... four... five legs. Mrs. Cauldwell, to your knowledge, of how many limbs was Bellerophon possessed?

MRS. CAULDWELL
Oh, this is gruesome. I can't stand it!

MRS. CAULDWELL exits. She goes to the hat-stand and puts on ASQUITH's shirtfront.

BEWLEY
Are you thinking what I'm thinking, Maurus?

MAURUS
It would be an honour if I were, Doctor.

BEWLEY
This would seem to confirm that the dog did not transform into something, but rather something turned into the dog. After treating the original rather badly.

ASQUITH [MRS. CAULDWELL] enters with a bucket.

ASQUITH [MRS. CAULDWELL]
The Nygard ice, sir.

MRS. COPPER [VAN WALL] *curtsies and exits.*

DON
Ugh. Give it to one of the egg-heads.

MAURUS
You know, you're a biologist too, Don.

DON
Well, yes, I've done the exams, but I didn't think I'd have to actually poke at anything! Besides: I could never be a scientist. I just can't stand working. I love having money and things, but I'd sooner slide slowly into ruin than have to have to participate in any of this. I have a note from mother that says I'm excused from "real life", and I assume something tragic will happen to me before the inheritance runs out. I'm going to check on old Aunt Aud.

DON exits. ASQUITH [MRS. CAULDWELL] follows, VAN WALL returns.

MAURUS
This is extraordinary, Dr. Bewley.

BEWLEY
Mm. They're like little worms or grubs.

VAN WALL
Be careful! If they did that to the dog, we should make sure they're dead! They're dangerous. What if they were to get at one of us?

MAC
What if they already have?

BEWLEY
Now let's not get excited. They're only tiny grubs they can't get out of the bucket. They should be studied.

VAN WALL
They should be exterminated!

MAC
Yes!

MAURUS
This is a decision we should all make together.

VAN WALL
It's an execution we should perform mercilessly and immediately. I'm going to find Don.

Exit VAN WALL.

BEWLEY
I'll see if I can find your mother. Maurus, you keep those safe, will you?

Exit BEWLEY.

MAC
Alone at last.

MAURUS
Yes. Listen, Mac... I tried to call you.

MAC
Oh, please, don't strain yourself.

MAURUS
It's only, our date... I had some misgivings... about exactly where we left things.

MAC
Surely not.

MAURUS
Now, haha. Yes. Look. What I mean to say is that I behaved badly and I'm sorry.

MAC
Um. Ok. Don't worry about it.

MAURUS

I quite understand that you want no more to do with me. And in fact, when Don invited me here this weekend, I very nearly declined, but I feel strongly that this sort of... reprehensible behaviour has been swept under the carpet for too long, and I wanted to make an apology in person. Now I feel like I misjudged it, and I've made you uncomfortable.

MAC

Um, not really. I'm fine. You're taking all this a bit hard, don't you think? People get carried away sometimes. Especially after a few drinks...

MAURUS

Oh. Huh.

MAC

What?

MAURUS

How can you not be angry!? Wait, no. Sorry. I don't want to tell you how to react...

MAC

It was a night out. Sometimes these thing happen.

MAURUS

Really?! No. I'm sorry. Of course you can think what you like, but I hold myself to a certain standard. I won't use drunkenness as an excuse. It's absolutely disgusting the way some men behave and it's been ignored and excused...

MAC

Sorry. I'm just... baffled. I'm not sure this is as significant as you're making out. I mean, so long as you don't make a habit of it... Maybe you're misremembering...

MAURUS

I'm not one of these fellows who is totally blind to social cues. Take Dr. Bewley for instance. A brilliant scientist, yes, but as a man... I wouldn't want to be anything like him.

MAC

... Has Dr. Bewley... done that sort of thing?

MAURUS

Mm... I'm afraid I've heard some stories. Only rumours of course, and he's retired now, so I don't imagine there will be any kind of scandal, but the word is that he can be a bit of an octopus.

MAC

... An octopus? Are they known for...? Never mind.

MAURUS

Regardless. I deeply regret my behaviour and I am very ashamed to learn that I have such an entitled and lecherous side to myself.

MAC

Lecherous?

MAURUS

Let's not mince words.

MAC

Waaait. What exactly is it that you think you did?

MAURUS

What... Well, I was distinctly... overly... forthright.

MAC

Maurus. Let's not mince words.

MAURUS

Alright! Alright. Tactile! I was downright tactile!

MAC

... Do... Do you mean that business with the arm around the waist?

MAURUS

Among other shameful violations of personal space.

MAC

Haha!

MAURUS

What? What?

MAC

Maurus. That was... that was fine.

MAURUS

Uh...

MAC

That's what you were worried about?

MAURUS

Should I not have been?

MAC

Not at all. Aw, Maurus. You may be exceptionally uptight, but in that context a little physical contact is perfectly normal, and... well... quite nice. I think even with your... peculiarly distorted concept of normality, it would have become quickly apparent to us both if you were less than a gentleman in that regard.

MAURUS

Oh... oh... so I wasn't... beastly.

MAC

Believe me. If you had deserved to be told off, I would not have waited this long.

MAURUS

Ah... Ah, good! ... But... but then, wait, what did you think we were talking about?

MAC

You don't remember? Later on in the evening?

MAURUS

Well... some of it's rather blurry, but...

MAC
>You did have quite a few cocktails.

MAURUS
>What did I do?

MAC
>How do I put this...? You... you defecated in a public dustbin.

MAURUS
>I what?!

MAC
>Haha!

Enter MRS. CAULDWELL, BEWLEY, DON, and VAN WALL.

MRS. CAULDWELL
>Well I'm glad someone is having a fine time. As for myself, my poor baby pup has been horribly slaughtered! And I demand that these hideous things should be executed for their crimes!

BEWLEY
>But Audrey, think what we might learn from such magical protean creatures!

MRS. CAULDWELL
>Sheri! How can you defend them! After what they did!

MAC
>My mother is right, those things may be small but they are deadly. What do you say, Don? Van Wall?

VAN WALL
>I don't understand why we haven't killed them already.

DON
>I think you're all missing the real issue here.

MAC
>What's that?

DON

>We are low on ice! After this bucket we shall be reduced to -
>   *He shudders.*
>- "neat" drinks. I don't wish to overstate things, but this is a
>catastrophe.

MRS. CAULDWELL

>Don! Would you desist!

DON

>Beg pardon?

MRS. CAULDWELL

>Must you insist on being so frivolous!

DON

>We are all slaves to our basic nature, dear aunt.

MAURUS

>I'm afraid it looks like everyone is agreed, doctor. They're too
>great a threat. We'll need to strain them out and burn them.

VAN WALL

>I'll get a sieve from the kitchen.

>*Exit VAN WALL, she puts on MRS. COPPER's chef's hat.*

BEWLEY

>It's a terrible loss, Audrey. The potential for what we could
>learn is astronomical, limitless, world-changing! But I respect
>your -

VAN WALL (off)

>Aaaauuughh! No Mrs. Copper! Get away from me! Shoo! No
>come back here! Where are you going?

>*Enter MRS. COPPER-MONSTER with a mutant arm.*

MRS. COPPER-MONSTER [VAN WALL]

>Glaauauuuughghhgh!

MAC grabs the fire iron and strikes MRS. COPPER-MONSTER in the head. The head appears to die, but the body does not fall.

A short movement sequence in which MRS. COPPER-MONSTER attacks the guests and is beaten down and burned. During the fight, MRS. COPPER-MONSTER's arm is severed. It comes to life on its own and must be killed again.

Act II

MRS. CAULDWELL, MAC, MAURUS, DON, VAN WALL, BEWLEY

DON mixes everyone drinks.

MRS. CAULDWELL
> Here is what we know: There is a creature loose. Possibly extra-terrestrial, probably other-worldly, certainly somewhat enterprising in its attitude to biology as we know it. It is able to perfectly imitate the form of animals and even humans, although it seems to take a little while to make the transformation. Am I correct so far?

BEWLEY
> Quite right, yes.

MRS. CAULDWELL
> Good. Now we know that it can only be rendered permanently... inert by burning.

MAURUS
> We've also seen, from the severed arm of the poor cook, that each part of the thing appears to have a life of its own, and will fight for survival.

VAN WALL
> But the dog, and all the little worms were accounted for when the cook was... contaminated! That means-

MAC
> Yes. There's still one of those things running loose.

MAURUS
> At least one.

VAN WALL
> It could be any one of us!

MRS. CAULDWELL
> Who was out of the room at the time?

VAN WALL
You were!

BEWLEY
And so were you, my dear.

MAURUS
And you and Don went out for a while too. I suppose that, since the creature attacked Mac, she must be... um... human.

MRS. CAULDWELL
Except that the two of you were left alone in here for... several minutes. Perhaps she was attacked again!

MAURUS
Now see here...

BEWLEY
If I may. Nobody seems to be behaving strangely. No more strangely than usual anyway.

VAN WALL
But no-one can entirely be accounted for. Everyone is a suspect.

DON
Oh! Marvelous!

BEWLEY puts on ASQUITH's shirtfront.

MAURUS
Um, Don, do you have any more... servants?

DON
Servants? Oh god, where's Asquith!?

ASQUITH [BEWLEY]
Here, sir.

DON
Asquith! Must you lurk in the shadows like that? Who else still works here?

ASQUITH [BEWLEY]
Following Mrs. Copper's untimely departure, only myself and Mrs. Navidson, sir. I shall fetch her, sir.

MAURUS
I'd better go with him.

MAURUS and ASQUITH [BEWLEY] exit.

DON
Oh god! Who's going to cook now?!

MAC
Don! More important things.

DON
Yes, yes. At least she went out on a good note. Those apricot things were lovely.

VAN WALL
And the nut roast was fabulous. Oh no! Did a monster make the nut-roast?!

MRS. CAULDWELL
No, if there's one thing we can say for certain, it's that the nut-roast was the work of a human being.

DON and MAC go to the hatstand. MAURUS and ASQUITH [BEWLEY] enter with MRS. NAVIDSON's wig and place it on DON.

MAC (wary)
Hello Mrs. Navidson.

MRS. NAVIDSON [DON]
H'lo miss. Is there something I can be helping you with?

MRS. CAULDWELL
You know Mrs. Navidson best, Asquith. Does she seem... usual.

ASQUITH [BEWLEY]
Madam, Mrs. Navidson is quite the most usual person I know.

VAN WALL

Are you mad, Asquith, look at her! She's a slavering space-beast! Underneath, probably.

MRS. CAULDWELL

How are you feeling, Mrs. Navidson?

MRS. NAVIDSON [DON]

Oh, you know how 'tis, Missus. C, I can't complain. Happy enough. Only when it's cold like this and I'm up and down about the house all day my feet do swell up something dreadful. I feel it in the joints terribly these days. The hip, the knee, and the lower back. You see I don't sleep awfully-

MRS. CAULDWELL

It's useless! If she's a forgery, she's a masterpiece! Someone in this room is certainly not who they seem, but evidently this creature can imitate not only the outward form, but also the persona of its victim.

BEWLEY removes ASQUITH's shirtfront and MRS. NAVIDSON's wig and hangs them back on the hatstand.

MAURUS

From now on I propose that we stay in groups of at least three.

MRS. CAULDWELL

I'm starting to have a plan. Mackenzie, dear, you're inappropriately capable when it comes to machinery and engines and things.

MAC

Mother!

MRS. CAULDWELL

Well it's quite unbecoming, but perhaps you can make yourself useful and cobble together some kind of... fire-machine. Something that we can use to eliminate these ghastly beasts, should they present themselves.

MAC

Mother, are you proposing that I go and build a flamethrower from things I can find about the house?

MRS. CAULDWELL
I don't see there's any need to be quite so dramatic about it.

MAC
No, no. Just some childhood fantasies being realized. Doctor, can I borrow you for this? And Don, you know where everything is.

Exit MAC, BEWLEY and DON.

MRS. CAULDWELL
So. You two. Mr. Maurus. I understand that you have intentions towards my daughter. Hand me that bucket would you?

Stunned, MAURUS hands her the ice-bucket. MRS. CAULDWELL arranges the bucket, a set of scalpels, and fresh napkins on a side table, and places an iron in the fire as the conversation continues.

MAURUS
What?! I - no... I mean, I wouldn't say... That is... we went on a... it's not... ahaa... Not that it's any of your... I mean... She... I don't think she... that she likes me very much.

MRS. CAULDWELL
Hm. Well perhaps the girl has some sense after all. In any case, I will thank you to stop leering at her. It's quite indecent the way you undress her with your eyes.

MAURUS
I... indecent?

MRS. CAULDWELL
And you. I see you persist in leading my poor nephew astray.

VAN WALL
Me! Leading *him* astray!

MRS. CAULDWELL
I don't know what the nature of your relationship to poor Donnie is, and I don't wish to know. The boy must be allowed his freedom, but it is quite plain to me that you are an

21

impediment to his happiness. You've become an albatross to him and the decent thing to do would be for you to jump ship as soon as possible.

VAN WALL
I... he's thirty-two!

MRS. CAULDWELL
All the more reason for him to settle down and find a wife.

VAN WALL
I'm fairly sure he's not planning to do that.

MRS. CAULDWELL
Not while you're following him around like some ghoulish lost puppy!

VAN WALL and MAURUS gape.

MRS. CAULDWELL
I don't wish to be unfair to you. You have a sense of your own worth, of course. My nephew considers you a dear friend, and my daughter has decided that you are an interesting prospect.

MAURUS
She has?!

MRS. CAULDWELL
So you will thank me for disabusing you of these silly notions. You are both utterly unsuitable companions. Unwanted, parasitic. And if you have any regard for Mackenzie and Don, you will discontinue this association as soon as possible.

VAN WALL
Um...

Enter BEWLEY, DON and MAC with a homemade flamethrower.

DON mixes drinks for everyone.

MAURUS
Ah! Oh thank god! That was awfully quick.

MAC

> To be honest it's not an eventuality that I had not pondered.

DON

> And not infrequently. Nor not in no little depth, neither.

MRS. CAULDWELL

> No. Now, I have arranged a simple and effective way of discerning which of us is one of those dreadful creatures. So everyone do as I say, and we shall have all this cleared up post-haste. We have here, a set of my nephew's scalpels. Each of us must commit a small amount of blood to this bucket, like so.

> *MRS. CAULDWELL slices her thumb, leaking a little blood into the bucket. Everyone winces. She staunches the cut with a napkin.*

MAC

> Mother! Have you lost your mind?

> *MAC puts down the flame-thrower.*

MRS. CAULDWELL

> Oh, don't be such a baby. Come, doctor, you go next.

> *BEWLEY follows her example.*

MAC

> But what is this going to achieve?

MRS. CAULDWELL

> I think that should be obvious. To us, blood is simply tissue. Once it's out of the body it's of no further interest. But each part of this nasty creature is a separate entity, and will try to preserve itself, to defend it's life.

DON

> I'm going to get this over with. Ow ow ow.

> *DON bleeds himself into the bucket.*

MRS. CAULDWELL
It will, for instance, crawl away from a red hot poker.

MRS. CAULDWELL retrieves the hot iron from the fire.

MAURUS
That's all very well Mrs. Cauldwell, but oughtn't the samples to be kept separate? For instance, in individually labelled petri dishes? Putting them all together in a big bucket will only tell us what we already know.

Pause. She thinks.

MRS. CAULDWELL
Drat. You're right.

MAC
You could have explained yourself before you barged ahead with it, mother. That is just absolutely like you.

MRS. CAULDWELL
Shut up, dear. Well, we might as well clear the three of us all at once. This is how the process will work. Hold the bucket, Don.

MAC picks up the flame-thrower. MRS. CAULDWELL places the tip of the fire iron into the bucket in DON's hands. As the tip of the iron touches the blood it transforms into a hideous blood-monster that writhes and screams, snapping its teeth. Everyone jumps back. DON holds the bucket at arm's length. He turns and casts it into the fire, where the screaming subsides.

Pause.

MRS. CAULDWELL
Oh dear.

VAN WALL
My god! It's one of them! One of them is the thing!

MAC
At least one of them. Oh, mother, you idiot.

MAC puts down the flame-thrower.

MRS. CAULDWELL
Well it can't be me! I came up with the idea!

DON
And made an absolute hash of it, I'm afraid.

BEWLEY
Now look here. I think this can be salvaged. Each of us still has a small blood sample here.

He holds up a blood-stained napkin.

MAURUS
Oh yes!

BEWLEY
If we set these alight, we will have a more accurate answer.

MAURUS
Yes. That'll work just the same.

MAC
Alright. Go ahead doctor.

MAC picks up the flame-thrower. BEWLEY places his napkin into the fire. No effect. Everyone is more comfortable with BEWLEY.

BEWLEY
Now be on your guards. The creature may react badly when it is exposed. Perhaps I should take the - um - since I am proven human.

MAC
Hm. Well... ok.

MAC grudgingly hands over the flamethrower.

BEWLEY
Donald?

DON cautiously steps forward.

DON
    I would... *know* if I *was* one... wouldn't I?

MAC & MAURUS
    Yes!

DON
    Yes, yes. Of course. Well. Cheerio.

    DON drops his napkin into the fire. No effect.

DON
    Phew!

    Everyone turns to MRS. CAULDWELL. Backing away slightly.

MRS. CAULDWELL
    Oh this is absolutely absurd.

MAURUS
    By a process of elimination, Mrs. Cauldwell...

MRS. CAULDWELL
    Honestly. Don't be so stupid.

    MRS. CAULDWELL flings her napkin into the flames. No effect.

MRS. CAULDWELL
    It must have learned not to react that way. That should have
    been a perfectly good test. I couldn't have known it wouldn't
    prove anything!

MAC
    But it did prove something, mother. Even if it only worked in
    that first instance, it proved - without a shadow of a doubt -
    that one of the three of you is not human.

VAN WALL
    Wait. Did it? How did it do that?

MAC
    Well, ordinary human blood doesn't tend to have teeth.
    Perhaps I should take that back now, doctor.

BEWLEY
Hm? Oh, yes. I suppose so.

BEWLEY passes the flamethrower to MAC. DON puts on MRS.
NAVIDSON's wig.

MAURUS
We're back to square one. Or damn near it.

MAC
It's alright. So long as we keep our nerve, and all remain watchful... we'll route out these things.

MAC puts down the flame-thrower.

MRS. NAVIDSON [DON]
What makes you think there's more than one?

VAN WALL
What makes you think there's not?!

MRS. NAVIDSON [DON]
I was only asking.

VAN WALL
That's what a monster would say! I don't like the way she's been looking at me all this time!

MRS. NAVIDSON [DON]
I'll look where I like.

VAN WALL
Has she been in the room this whole time? I don't even know, the little viper!

BEWLEY
Now, let's not lose our heads.

MRS. CAULDWELL
I should say we are in danger of losing more than our heads!

MRS. NAVIDSON [DON]
Maybe *I* don't like the way she's looking at *me*!

MAURUS
We just need to look at this logically. Scientifically.

MAC
Ok! So let's take Mrs. Navidson as a test subject.

MRS. NAVIDSON [DON]
Why not her!?

MAC
Please. Mrs. Navidson. If you could just answer a few questions. We can establish your innocence. For instance... let's start simple. Your son's name.

MRS. NAVIDSON [DON]
Oh fine. It's Paul.

MRS. CAULDWELL
Very good. And... what instrument did Don play as a child.

MRS. NAVIDSON [DON]
Oh, he took up the clarinet. But he only carried it around the summer, I don't know I ever saw him play the thing.

VAN WALL
Mm. That's very accurate, I don't see that it proves anything, though. How about this. How did Dr. Maurus come to be part of our set?

MRS. NAVIDSON [DON]
Oh, well, Dr. Maurus was a student with Mr. Stuart. They became friends at university.

MAURUS
Quite right.

MRS. NAVIDSON [DON]
But I doubt he would have been invited this weekend, if Mr. Stuart weren't looking to pair him up with Miss Cauldwell here. In fact it was at Miss Cauldwell's suggestion that-

MAC
> What?! No I don't think that's-

MAURUS
> No, no. Go on. What was at Miss Cauldwell's -

VAN WALL
> This is pointless! Why are we gossiping with this thing when we should be burning it!

Following lines all spoken overlapping.

BEWLEY
> This line of questioning is clearly-

MRS. NAVIDSON [DON]
> Burning! Oh, you little minx, I've never in my life-

MRS. CAULDWELL
> We have to establish how perfect it's imitation.

MAURUS
> Perhaps it would be best-

MAC
> If you would all just stop for a-

VAN WALL kills MRS. NAVIDSON [DON] with a scalpel.

MRS. NAVIDSON [DON]
> Aarg! She's stabbed me! Murderer. Murr...

MRS. NAVIDSON dies. DON transfers the wig to BEWLEY who lies down as the body.

MAC
> Van! What...
> *MAC wrestles the scalpel from a stunned VAN WALL*

VAN WALL
> Oh... I was sure she was one of them.

DON

My word Van. You've gone and killed my housekeeper. I'll have no staff left!

VAN WALL

I didn't mean to.

MRS. CAULDWELL

That did not look very accidental.

VAN WALL

I mean... I thought she was...

A movement set-piece. The body reanimates, transforming into a horrible monster. It thrashes around. The guests frantically try to defend themselves as they move behind MAC. MAC uses the flamethrower, killing the monster.

Act III

MAC, MAURUS, DON, VAN WALL, MRS. CAULDWELL, BEWLEY.

DON mixes drinks for everyone.

MAC

There was something about Mrs. Navidson. Something unusual.

MAURUS

Oh. What gave it away? The flailing tentacles or... ?

MAC

Before that. Her behaviour. The way she spoke.

DON

Oh, she was absolutely shameless. She's normally - or she was normally - a perfectly meek little thing. Even during her frequent panics. She's often angry, but she certainly never forgets her place.

MAC

That's it! At least it's worth a try. It may have learned to look and sound like us, but I suspect it has a little more trouble falling into our social conventions. Which things should be said and which should be kept quiet.

MAURUS

So all we have to do is coax each of us in turn towards a social blunder. Towards saying something we shouldn't. Anyone foolish enough to brazenly commit a faux-pas, rather than nimbly circumnavigate, is not human.

MAC

Although with you, I'm not convinced it will work, judging by the sort of things you were saying to me the other night - when you were certainly most dreadfully human.

MAURUS

I! But you said...

MRS. CAULDWELL

What!? What exactly were you saying to my daughter the other night Mr. Maurus?!

MAURUS

Ah! What? Nothing. I mean. I'm not sure this is appropriate... conversation just now... given the...

MAC

You're quite right, Maurus. But I've just demonstrated my test. You blushed a very human shade. Either the test is a dud, or, with that desperate scrabble for dignity, you're in the clear.

MAURUS

Oh. I see. Quite unpleasant. Well... perhaps you could at least put me out of my misery and tell me plainly what you thought of our evening together.

MAC

Oh I wouldn't wish to spoil the mystery.

MAURUS

Which suggests that, if you are a monster, at least your the human sort.

DON

Oh this is sensational. Do me next.

BEWLEY

Now won't the creature simply learn to keep its trap shut? It adapted before. It might again. Then we're right back where we started.

MAURUS

It's possible. But then we'd be sure to suspect anyone who's too cagey. The creature may simply not perceive the difference between what is acceptable and what is not. It's like testing someone for colour-blindness. What is utterly plain to all of us could be genuinely invisible to the creature.

BEWLEY

Hm. I suppose it could work. Now, I don't wish to criticize - as a human myself, I wish to do nothing but facilitate - but without a positive result it all seems rather hypothetical.

MAC

But if it can be proven to work, and both of you are cleared, then you and my mother can continue whatever peculiar geriatric romance you are pursuing.

BEWLEY

Haha! Oh, romance? No. I see you're trying to test me, but - ha - nothing of the sort.

MAC

Ah. Good.

BEWLEY

No. I prefer the young models, if you know what I mean.

BEWLEY pinches VAN WALL - she jumps, affronted. Everyone turns on BEWLEY.

BEWLEY

You know, Maurus. It's... what's wrong?

MAC picks up the flamethrower.

BEWLEY

Now see here...

A beat, then BEWLEY expands into a gruesome monster.

BEWLEY-MONSTER

I AM MEDICAL PROFESSIONAL WITH CREDENTIALS OF THE HIGHEST CALIBER! I WILL NOT HAVE MY CHARACTER IMPUGNED IN THIS MANNER! HOW DARE YOU CAST ASPERSIONS ON MY REPUTATION! THIS BEHAVIOUR IS QUITE UNACCEPTABLE...!

The others are ready this time and MAC incinerates him with the flamethrower.

MRS. CAULDWELL
Sheri! I can't believe it!

MAC sets down the flame-thrower.

DON
Yes, poor old Doctor Bewley. Still. Test seems to work.

DON mixes drinks for everyone.

VAN WALL
Rather an undignified end to the wretched man. Not that he hasn't misbehaved before... but in public like that...

MRS. CAULDWELL
It's possible, though, that he was the only one. But how can we clear the rest of us? I for one, have no dirty secrets of hidden agendas that I would hesitate to speak aloud. I don't see that your test could possibly work on me.

VAN WALL
Well, romance does seem to be the topic of choice. I think I should be revealed as a monster immediately if I were, for instance to disclose the details of Don's love-life.

DON freezes.

DON
Oh, don't you dare, you profane little scorpion!

VAN WALL
A very human objection, Don. Well done.

DON
Hm? Oh. I see. Well, I suppose... alright then.

DON resumes mixing drinks for everyone.

MAURUS
And, Ms. Van Wall, I think your choice of subjects there accounts for you too. You knew just where he line was.

DON
> No one can nettle like Van.

VAN WALL
> You're welcome.

MAC
> And now mother.

> *Everyone looks at MRS. CAULDWELL suspiciously.*

MRS. CAULDWELL
> I'm telling you it won't work.

MAC
> Perhaps you're worried that you'll fall for the same trap Dr. Bewley did. It's clear that you had feelings for him.

MRS. CAULDWELL
> And why shouldn't I, precisely? Can't a poor widow enjoy the company of a gentleman? There was absolutely nothing untoward about my friendship with the doctor - notwithstanding his own weaknesses.

> *Everyone sighs, dissatisfied.*

DON
> I'm still a little on the fence. She has such poise, you see.

MRS. CAULDWELL
> Oh, darling nephew, stop.

DON
> You stop.

MAC
> She's being deliberately awkward. She's jealous that she's not in control anymore. She resents my taking charge.

MRS. CAULDWELL
> Don't be ridiculous, you stupid girl.

General shrugs. DON resumes mixing drinks for everyone. MAURUS
looks into the fire. MAC kicks at the floor.

MRS. CAULDWELL
I'm very proud of you.

Everyone freezes.

MAC
You're... what?

MRS. CAULDWELL
Are you deaf? I said I'm pr- ... Oh... Damn.

Movement set piece. MRS. CAULDWELL expands into a monster.
MAC freezes up and cannot use the flamethrower. MRS.
CAULDWELL-MONSTER attacks. The remaining guests dodge out of
the way. VAN WALL drags MAC to safety. MAURUS takes the
flamethrower and finally incinerates MRS. CAULDWELL-MONSTER.

Act IV

MAC, MAURUS, DON, VAN WALL

DON mixes drinks for everyone.

MAURUS
>	Well. We'd better finish up. We still have to test the butler.

DON
>	Asquith! Of course! He'll definitely be one, that demon! Where's he gone!?

MAURUS
>	Isn't he...?

DON
>	That phantom! How does he do it!?

MAC
>	How could you let him escape like that?

DON
>	He's always been slippery! He seems to fade into invisibility whenever he's not speaking!

MAURUS
>	We'd better go looking for him. Mac, maybe you should come with me.

MAC
>	Yes. I... I'll be alright, but it would be good to get out of this room...

MAURUS
>	You two stay here in case he turns up.

Exit MAC and MAURUS.

DON

All in all, not my finest weekend in the country. I'm sorry, Liz. Sorry to drag you into all this, you know. Exposing you to... my aunt... and death.

VAN WALL

That's alright. You couldn't have known.

DON

Well, not the monsters and so on, but I had a fair idea how Aunt Aud would behave. When she was Aunt Aud. Only, the thing is, I don't think I could manage any of this sort of thing without you here to help me. I don't know how to speak to any of these people - they seem a completely alien species to me.

VAN WALL

How apt. And anyway you seem very much at ease. You're a natural host.

DON

Only when there's someone else here to witness the awfulness of it all. Van, you're aware of it in a way that the rest of them simply aren't. Monsters or not. All their sordid reality.

VAN WALL

Yes. Well you and I are not like them, Don. I'm not sure how they manage it.

DON

What exactly is it that they are managing, do you think?

VAN WALL

Hope, I think. A kind of belief in themselves. That they can solve things and that it matters. That they can save the world. That any of it means anything.

DON

Oh. That's rather a downer. If hope is the thing I can't stand.

VAN WALL

I'm afraid it might be.

DON
> I suppose it fits. I may not be a magical shape-changing monster, but people like me are certainly not much of a benefit to anyone.

VAN WALL
> Please, Don. You mean people like *us*.

Pause. Smile.

Enter MAC and MAURUS.

MAC
> The house is empty.

DON
> Hm... Wait!...Look! There's a light in the shed!

MAURUS
> You're right. Stay here.

DON
> No, no. Our turn. Van. Let's make ourselves useful for once!

Exit DON and VAN WALL. VAN WALL grabs ASQUITH's shirt front as the dash out.

MAURUS
> Alone at last.

Beat.

MAURUS
> Wonder what's got into them.

MAC
> You don't need to tread on eggshells around me, Maurus.

MAURUS
> I'm sorry. It's just. She was your mother.

MAC

> Yes. And I'm upset. But there will be time for that later.
> Anyhow, she was closer with Don than she was with me really.
> Silly old bag.

> *MAC smiles sadly. MAURUS sits by her.*

MAC

> The Thing must have got her a while ago. I wonder which
> conversation was the last one I had with my real mother.

MAURUS

> She was very protective of you. You should have heard what
> she said to me earlier. And even that grotesque copy knew
> that she was proud of you. That must have been true.

MAC

> Mm. That's the most upsetting part.

> *A moment together.*

> *Enter DON, beaming, pushing ASQUITH [VAN WALL] and dragging
> in a MAGICAL SLEDGE.*

DON

> Got him! And look at what he was building out there! No need
> to test this little lizard.

ASQUITH [VAN WALL]

> I'm afraid you have the wrong end of the stick sir.

MAURUS

> Where's Van Wall?

DON

> Oh, damn. She must have got lost. It's quite a blizzard out
> there. We can go find her after this monster is dealt with. Look
> as his magic chariot! What are these? Druidic symbols?
> Witchcraft? Moonman language?

ASQUITH [VAN WALL]

> It's a perfectly innocent carpentry project, sir. I do have
> hobbies.

DON
>It's no good Asquith! I saw it glowing. The jig is up.

ASQUITH [VAN WALL]
>Really, sir... well, then... if that's what you think...

ASQUITH [VAN WALL] runs away. Exit. The others are surprised.

DON
>Oh. I thought he was going to do the other thing.

MAC
>Stay here and wait for Van Wall. We'll get him.

>*MAC and MAURUS run out.*

DON is left alone. Short clown sequence in which DON clears up his living room and mixes drinks for everyone with the last of the ice.

DON
>That's it. No more ice.

>*Enter VAN WALL. They look at each other in silence.*

>*Enter MAC with ASQUITH [MAURUS] by the arm.*

MAC
>Come on.

DON
>What ho, Mac. What happened to Maurus?

MAC
>He was right there a second ago. Let's get rid of this one first.

DON
>Ah. And you've decided to do that inside the house. Ok.

MAC
>We wouldn't want the neighbours to see.

>*MAC shoves ASQUITH [MAURUS] to the center of the room.*

ASQUITH [MAURUS]
   You may consider this my notice, siiieaaargh!

ASQUITH [MAURUS] transforms and MAC torches him. DON ends standings by MAC, VAN WALL further off:

Pause.

VAN WALL
   Step away from him, Mac. He's one of them now.

MAC
   What?

VAN WALL
   I got lost in the snow for a moment. Don found Asquith on his own. It was just the two of them. I wasn't quick enough. I saw. And now... now... That's not Don. That's not my Don.

MAC
   Don?

Movement piece. DON suddenly pushes MAC to the ground. He leaps across the room, growing into a grotesque monster. He half-devours VAN WALL. Eating her alive.

MAC recovers, turns to face them. She can't get a clear shot at the monster. A moment of clarity between MAC and VAN WALL. It's too late to save her. MAC incinerates them both. The DON-MONSTER reaches out with the last of its strength and destroys the flamethrower.

Epilogue

MAC

MAC pours herself a neat whisky from a large green J&B bottle.

Enter MAURUS.

MAC
    Where did you get off to? You missed all the fun.

MAURUS
    I'm sorry. I... I got turned around. The snow.

MAC
    Just you and me now. Alone at last.

MAURUS
    What happened to the fire-machine?

MAC
    It's broken. But even if it worked, I don't think I'd be able to tell
    if you were one of those things. Not just between the two of us.

MAURUS
    Nor I you. What now?

MAC
    Would you like a drink?

*As MAC pours a drink for MAURUS and hands it to him, their
movements slow to a gelatinous pace of the Prelude, and the light
fades. The other performers re-enter and they all dance slowly, as
character and scene dissolve.*

THE END

JAMES CARNEY

Printed in Poland
by Amazon Fulfillment
Poland Sp. z o.o., Wrocław